Contents

KU-274-922

Waiter

Edward is pretending
to be a waiter.
He is serving some
play food to his toys.

Let's pretend we are...

Pe
W

Karen B

Leamington Library
Royal Pump Rooms
The Parade
Royal Leamington Spa
CV32 4AA
Tel 01926 742721/2
Renewals 01926 742720
Fax 01926 742743

4/04
28. MAY 04
22. JUN 05
2 3 MAY 2008
1 7 NOV 2008
13 JUL 2009

p10709

This item is to be returned on or before the latest date above.
... rowed for a further period if not in demand .

Warwickshire
County Council

...tage · Trading Standards

DISCARDED

WARWICKSHIRE
COUNTY LIBRARY

...TROL No.
J331·7

0126053770

Heinemann
LIBRARY

First published in Great Britain by Heinemann Library, Halley Court, Jordan Hill, Oxford OX2 8EJ,
a division of Reed Educational & Professional Publishing Ltd.

OXFORD FLORENCE PRAGUE MADRID ATHENS MELBOURNE AUCKLAND KUALA LUMPUR
SINGAPORE TOKYO IBADAN NAIROBI KAMPALA JOHANNESBURG GABORONE
PORTSMOUTH NH (USA) CHICAGO MEXICO CITY SAO PAULO

© BryantMole Books 1998

All rights reserved. No part of this publication may be reproduced, stored in a retrieval system, or transmitted
in any form or by any means, electronic, mechanical, photocopying, recording, or otherwise without either
the prior written permission of the Publishers or a licence permitting restricted copying in the United
Kingdom issued by the Copyright Licensing Agency Ltd, 90 Tottenham Court Road, London W1P 9HE.

Designed by Jean Wheeler

Commissioned photography by Zul Mukhida

Produced by Colourpath Ltd., Soho.

Printed and bound in Hong Kong / China

03
10 9 8 7 6 5 4

ISBN 0 431 04653 0

This title is also available in a hardback library edition (ISBN 0 431 04652 2).

British Library Cataloguing in Publication Data
Bryant-Mole, Karen
Let's pretend we are people who help
1.Human services - Juvenile literature
2.Readers (Primary)
I.Title II.People who help
360

Words that appear in the text **in bold** can be found in the glossary.

Acknowledgements
The Publishers would like to thank the following for permission to reproduce photographs. Chapel
Studios; 5 Zul Mukhida, Eye Ubiquitous; 11 Matthew McKee, Positive Images; 17, Tony Stone Images; 7
Arthur Tilley, 9 Tim Brown, 13 David Paterson, 15 Kathi Lamm, 21 Mike Abrahams, 23 Jon Riley, Zefa; 19.

Every effort has been made to contact copyright holders of any material reproduced in this book.
Any omissions will be rectified in subsequent printings if notice is given to the Publisher.

The customers in this restaurant are choosing food from the **menu**.
The waitress writes down their order on a notepad.

Teacher

Megan is pretending
to teach maths to
her toys.
She has written some
adding up sums on
a **chalkboard**.

This teacher is teaching maths using
a computer program.
The children type in their answers using
a **keyboard**.

Dentist

Naheed has dressed up
as a dentist.
He is showing his little sister,
Alysha, how to brush her
teeth properly.

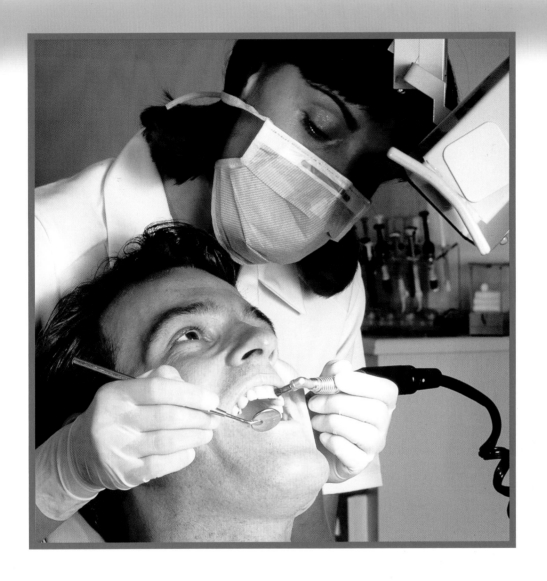

This dentist is using a special brush to polish
her patient's teeth.
She uses a tiny mirror to see behind
his teeth.

Postal worker

William's big bag holds lots of letters. He is delivering one of the letters to his friend, Edward.

Letters have to be sorted before
they can be delivered.
This postal worker is loading letters
onto a sorting machine.

Fire fighter

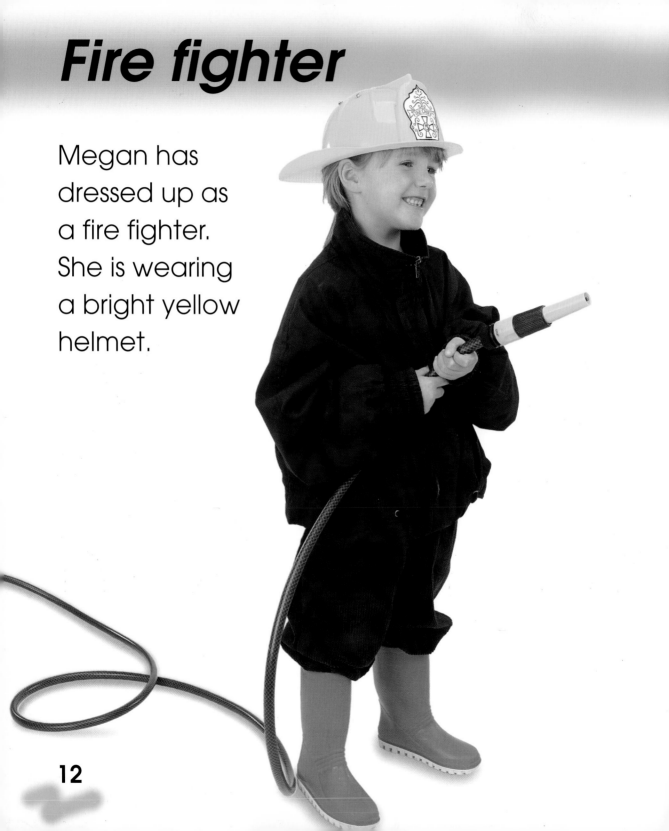

Megan has dressed up as a fire fighter. She is wearing a bright yellow helmet.

Being a fire fighter can be a dangerous job.
Fire fighters wear helmets to protect
their heads and special suits to protect
their bodies.

Vet

Naheed is pretending to be a vet visiting a farm. The duck has hurt its head.

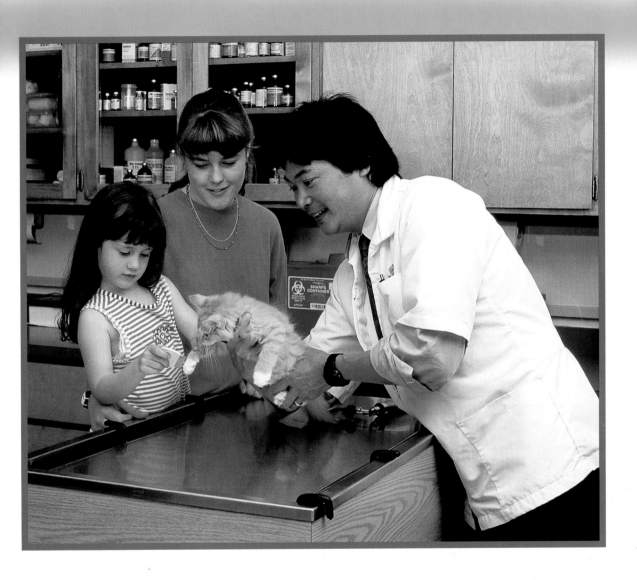

As well as looking after farm animals,
vets also look after our pets.
These girls have brought their kitten
to see the vet.

Police officer

Aliyu is speaking into a **walkie-talkie**. He is pretending to talk to another police officer.

This police officer is using a special car telephone. Police officers need to be able to keep in touch with one another.

Doctor

Emily is pretending that her teddy has a bad cough. She is using a **stethoscope** to listen to his breathing.

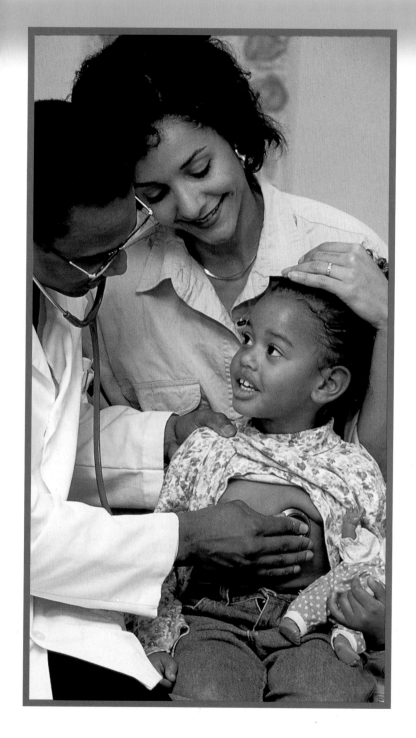

This doctor
is using his
stethoscope
to listen to a
little girl's heart.
He is making
sure that the
girl is healthy.

Nurse

Alysha is pretending to be a nurse in an operating theatre.
She is getting the patient ready for her operation.

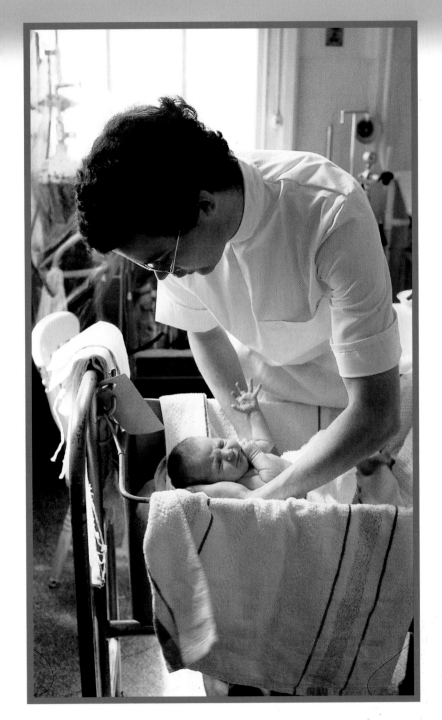

Nurses can choose the type of nursing they do. This man has chosen to work with newborn babies.

Librarian

Melissa is pretending to be a librarian.
She is helping Megan to find
a good book to read.

All the books in this library are listed
on computers.
The librarian can find books quickly
and easily.

Glossary

chalkboard a board that you can write on with chalk and then wipe clean

keyboard a control pad for a computer

menu a list of food that can be ordered

stethoscope an instrument used for listening to sounds inside your body

walkie-talkie a type of radio that people can use to talk to each other

Index